FRUIT DESSERTS
easy recipes
for beginners

by Michelle Desire

Table of contents

9

GRILLED PINK GRAPEFRUIT

(Serves 4)

Ingredients

- 2 pink grapefruit.
- 1 teaspoon granulated sugar.
- 4 scoops vanilla ice cream.

Procedure

1. Halve the grapefruit and cut round the edge of each, between the pith and the flesh. Separate the segments. Sprinkle each grapefruit with sugar.
2. Put in ramekins to keep them flesh side up, and put on a grill pan. Grill for 2–3 minutes until starting to lightly brown. Put a scoop of vanilla ice cream on top of each, and serve immediately.

LIME SHERBET

(Serves 4)

Ingredients

- 8 limes.
- 75g/3oz caster sugar.
- pinch of salt.
- crushed ice, to serve.

Procedure

1. Squeeze the limes and pour the juice into a large jug. Add the sugar and salt. Stir until dissolved

2. Pour in 1.5 litres/21/2pt water, and top up with plenty of ice to serve.

MANDARINS IN SYRUP

(Serves 4)

Ingredients

- 10 mandarin oranges.
- 15g/1/2oz icing sugar.
- 2 teaspoons orange-flower water.
- 15g/1/2oz chopped pistachio nuts.

Procedure

1. Thinly pare a little of the zest from 1 mandarin, and cut into fine shreds for decoration. Squeeze the juice from 2 mandarins and set aside;

2. Peel the remaining mandarins, removing as much of the white pith as possible. Arrange the peeled fruit whole in a large glass dish;

3. Mix the reserved mandarin juice, sugar and orange-flower water, and pour it over the fruit. Cover the dish and chill for at least an hour;

4. Blanch the shreds of mandarin zest in boiling water for 30 seconds. Drain and leave to cool;

5. To serve, sprinkle the shreds of zest and pistachio nuts over the mandarins, and serve immediately.

FRESH FIGS IN WINE

(Serves 6)

Ingredients

- 450ml/3/4pt dry white wine.
- 75g/3oz clear honey.
- 50g/2oz caster sugar.
- 1 small orange.
- 8 whole cloves.
- 450g/1lb fresh figs.
- 1 cinnamon stick.

Procedure

1. Put the wine, honey and sugar in a heavy saucepan, and heat gently until the sugar dissolves;

2. Stud the orange with the cloves, and add to the syrup with the figs and cinnamon. Cover and simmer until the figs are soft;

3. Transfer to a serving dish, and leave to cool before serving.

ORANGE & DATE SALAD

(Serves 6)

Ingredients

- 6 oranges.
- 2 tablespoons orange-flower water.
- 100g/4oz stoned dates, chopped.
- 50g/2oz pistachio nuts, chopped.
- 15g/1/2oz icing sugar.
- 1 teaspoon toasted almonds.

Procedure

1. Peel the oranges with a sharp knife, removing all the pith. Cut into segments, catching all the juice in a bowl. Put the segments in a serving dish.
2. Stir in the juice from the bowl and the orange-flower water.
3. Sprinkle the dates and nuts over the salad, along with the icing sugar. Chill for 1 hour.
4. Just before serving, sprinkle with the toasted almonds.

CALIFORNIAN BAKED PEARS

(Serves 4)

Ingredients

- 25g/1oz butter.
- 1 teaspoon granulated sugar..
- grated zest of 1/2 lemon.
- 4 dessert pears.
- 300g/11oz canned fruit cocktail in syrup.
- 1/2 teaspoon mixed spice.

Procedure

1. Preheat the oven to 190°C/375°F/Gas mark 5;
2. Melt the butter in a flameproof casserole dish. Add the sugar and lemon zest. Peel the pears, and turn in this mixture. Cover and bake for 30 minutes;
3. Add the fruit cocktail and its syrup, and sprinkle with the mixed spice. Return to the oven for 10 minutes;
4. Lift the pears out onto warmed plates. Stir the fruit cocktail well into the pan juices. Spoon around the pears, and serve immediately.

BANANA SPLIT

(Serves 4)

Ingredients

- 200g/7oz dark chocolate (at least 70% cocoa solids).
- 175ml/6fl oz double cream.
- 25g/1oz butter.
- 4 bananas.
- 12 scoops vanilla ice cream.
- mixed chopped nuts, to serve.

Procedure

1. Put the chocolate, cream and butter in a pan, and stir over a low heat until smooth. Cool slightly;

2. Split the bananas in half lengthways, and arrange in four glass dishes. Put 3 scoops of ice cream in each dish, and pour the chocolate sauce over the top;

3. Sprinkle with the chopped nuts, and serve immediately.

SUMMER BERRIES IN CHAMPAGNE JELLY

(Serves 8)

Ingredients

- 900ml/11/2pt Champagne.
- 11/2 teaspoons powdered gelatine.
- 250g/9oz granulated sugar.
- 250g/9oz strawberries, hulled and chopped.
- 250g/9oz blueberries.

Procedure

1. Pour half of the champagne into a large bowl, and let the bubbles subside. Sprinkle the gelatine over the top in an even layer. Do not stir. Leave until the gelatine is spongy;

2. Pour the remaining Champagne into a large saucepan, add the sugar and heat gently, stirring constantly, until all the sugar has dissolved. Remove the pan from the heat, add the gelatine mixture and stir until thoroughly dissolved. Cool completely;

3. Divide the berries among eight 125ml/4fl oz stemmed wine glasses, and gently pour the jelly over them. Chill in the refrigerator until set. Remove from the refrigerator 15 minutes before serving.

MANGO & MELON GINGER SALAD

(Serves 4)

Ingredients

- 2 avocados, peeled, stoned and flesh cut into slices.
- 1 mango, peeled and cut into slices.
- 1 cantaloupe melon, peeled and cut into slices.
- Grated zest and juice of 2 limes.
- 100g/4oz Stilton cheese, crumbled.
- 2 tablespoons finely chopped stem ginger.
- 2 passion fruit, halved.

Procedure

1. Arrange the slices of avocado, mango and melon decoratively on a serving plate.

2. Sprinkle the fruit with the lime zest and juice, Stilton and ginger. Spoon the passion fruit over the salad and serve.

MUSCAT GRAPE FRAPPÉ

(Serves 4)

Ingredients

- 1/2 bottle Muscat wine.
- 450g/1lb Muscat grapes.

Procedure

1. Pour the wine into a stainless-steel baking tray, add 150ml/5fl oz water and freeze for 3 hours or until completely solid;

2. Scrape the frozen wine with a tablespoon to make a fine ice. Combine the grapes with the ice, and spoon into four shallow glasses. Serve immediately.

SUMMER FRUITS WITH
RICOTTA & VANILLA DIP

(Serves 4)

Ingredients

- 250g/9oz ricotta cheese.
- 250g/9oz mascarpone cheese.
- 150ml/5fl oz crème fraiche.
- a few drops of vanilla essence.
- grated zest of 1 lemon.
- 50g/2oz caster sugar.
- 900g/2lb mixed fresh summer berries.

Procedure

- Beat the cheeses together with the crème fraîche, vanilla essence, lemon zest and sugar. Spoon into a serving dish, cover and chill for at least 30 minutes;
- To serve, pile the berries onto a serving plate, and spoon the ricotta and vanilla dip on top.

MULLED FLORIDA COCKTAIL

(Serves 6)

Ingredients

- 2 grapefruit.
- 2 oranges.
- 150ml/5fl oz apple juice.
- 1 tablespoon brandy.
- 2 fresh cherries, pitted and halved.

Procedure

1. Over a saucepan to catch the juice, remove all zest and pith from the grapefruit and oranges, and separate each into segments;

2. Put the segments in the saucepan. Add the apple juice and brandy. Heat through until almost boiling.

3. Spoon into four glass dishes and top each with half a cherry. Serve warm.

ETON MESS

(Serves 4)

Ingredients

- 150ml/5fl oz double cream, lightly whipped.
- 200ml/7fl oz Greek-style yogurt.
- 500g/1lb 2oz strawberries, hulled.
- 2 tablespoons crème de cassis.
- 5 meringue nests.

Procedure

1. Fold the cream into the yogurt and chill for 30 minutes;

2. Put 250g/9oz strawberries in a blender or food processor, blend to a purée, then stir in the crème de cassis. Measure out 75ml/3fl oz of the purée and reserve;

3. Slice the remaining strawberries into a bowl, reserving 6 for decoration, then pour the purée over and chill in the bowl for 20 minutes;

4. Break up the meringue nests, and carefully fold into the cream mixture along with the strawberry mixture. Divide between six serving glasses, then drizzle over the reserved purée;

5. Decorate with the reserved strawberries, and serve.

STRAWBERRIES ROMANOFF

(Serves 4)

Ingredients

- 750g/1lb 11oz strawberries, quartered.
- 2 tablespoons Cointreau.
- 1/2 teaspoon finely grated.
- orange zest.
- 15g/1/2oz caster sugar.
- 125ml/4fl oz double cream.
- 20g/3/4oz icing sugar.

Procedure

1. Combine the strawberries, Cointreau, orange zest and caster sugar in a large bowl, cover and refrigerate for 1 hour. Drain the strawberries, reserving any juices;

2. Purée about a quarter of the strawberries with the reserved juices in a blender or food processor. Divide the remaining strawberries among four glasses;

3. Beat the cream and icing sugar until soft peaks form, then fold the strawberry purée through the whipped cream. Spoon the mixture over the top of the strawberries, cover and refrigerate until needed.

SUMMER FRUITS WITH RICOTTA & VANILLA DIP

(Serves 6)

Ingredients

- 250g/9oz ricotta cheese.
- 250g/9oz mascarpone cheese.
- 150ml/5fl oz crème fraiche.
- a few drops of vanilla essence.
- grated zest of 1 lemon.
- 50g/2oz caster sugar.
- 900g/2lb mixed fresh summer berries.

Procedure

1. Beat the cheeses together with the crème fraîche, vanilla essence, lemon zest and sugar. Spoon into a serving dish, cover and chill for at least 30 minutes;
2. To serve, pile the berries onto a serving plate, and spoon the ricotta and vanilla dip on top.

STRAWBERRIES ROMANOFF

(Serves 4)

Ingredients

- 750g/1lb 11oz strawberries, quartered.
- 2 tablespoons Cointreau.
- 1/2 teaspoon finely grated.
- orange zest.
- 15g/1/2oz caster sugar.
- 125ml/4fl oz double cream.
- 20g/3/4oz icing sugar.

Procedure

1. Combine the strawberries, Cointreau, orange zest and caster sugar in a large bowl, cover and refrigerate for 1 hour. Drain the strawberries, reserving any juices;

2. Purée about a quarter of the strawberries with the reserved juices in a blender or food processor. Divide the remaining strawberries among four glasses;

3. Beat the cream and icing sugar until soft peaks form, then fold the strawberry purée through the whipped cream. Spoon the mixture over the top of the strawberries, cover and refrigerate until needed.

BANANAS WITH CHOCOLATE MARSHMALLOW SAUCE

(Serves 4)

Ingredients

- 4 slightly unripe bananas.
- 50g/2oz chocolate chips.
- 24 mini marshmallows.

Procedure

1. Preheat the oven to 160°C/325°F/Gas mark 3.

2. Trim the ends of the bananas, leaving on the skins. Using a sharp knife, make a lengthways slit in each one;

3. Gently prise open each banana, and fill with chocolate chips and marshmallows, then wrap each banana in foil. Bake in the oven for 15–20 minutes, and serve hot.

PINEAPPLE FLAMBÉ

(Serves 4)

Ingredients

- 1 large ripe pineapple, about 600g/11/4lb.
- 25g/1oz butter.
- 50g/2oz soft brown sugar.
- 50ml/2fl oz freshly squeezed orange juice.
- 25ml/1fl oz vodka.
- 1 tablespoon slivered almonds, toasted.

Procedure

- Cut away the top and base of the pineapple, then cut down the sides, removingNall the dark 'eyes'. Cut the pineapple into thin slices. Using an apple corer, remove the hard, central core from each slice;

- Melt the butter in a frying pan with the sugar. Add the orange juice and stir until hot. Add as many pineapple slices as the pan will hold, and cook for 1-2 minutes, turning once. As each pineapple slice browns, remove to a plate;

- Return all the pineapple slices to the pan, heat briefly, then pour over the vodka and carefully light with a long match. Let the flames die down, then sprinkle with the almonds and serve at once.

SPICED FRUIT PLATTER

(Serves 6)

Ingredients

- 1 pineapple
- 2 papayas
- 1 small cantaloupe melon
- juice of 2 limes
- 2 pomegranates
- chat masala, to taste

Procedure

1. Cut away the top and base of the pineapple, then cut down the sides, removing all the dark 'eyes'. Cut the pineapple into thin slices. Using an apple corer, remove the hard, central core from each slice;

2. Peel the papayas. Cut them in half, then into thin wedges. Halve the melon and remove the seeds from the middle. Cut into thin wedges and remove the skin;

3. Arrange the fruit on six individual plates, and sprinkle with the lime juice. Cut the pomegranates in half, and scoop out the seeds, discarding any bitter pith. Scatter the seeds over the fruit;

4. Serve, sprinkled with a little chat masala to taste.

GRILLED FRESH FIGS
WITH CRÉME FRAÎCHE

(Serves 4)

Ingredients

- 8 ripe fresh figs.
- 225g/8oz créme fraiche.
- 50g/2oz light muscovado sugar.

Procedure

1. Preheat the grill to high. Lightly butter a shallow flameproof dish, large enough to accommodate the figs in a single layer.

2. Cut the figs into quarters without cutting through the base, and gently open each one out a little. Spoon a dollop of crème fraîche into the centre of each fig.

3. Sprinkle the sugar evenly between the figs. Put the figs in the prepared dish, and put the hot grill for 2 minutes or until the sugar has melted and the crème fraîche starts to run. Serve immediately.

POACHED ALLSPICE PEARS

(Serves 4)

Ingredients

- 4 large dessert pears, peeled, cored and halved.
- 300ml/10fl oz orange juice.
- 2 teaspoons ground allspice.
- 50g/2oz raisins.
- 25g/1oz Demerara sugar.

Procedure

1. Put the pears in a large saucepan. Add the orange juice, ground allspice, raisins and sugar, and heat gently, stirring, until the sugar has dissolved. Bring the mixture to the boil and continue to boil for 1 minute.

2. Reduce the heat to low, and leave to simmer for about 10 minutes. Test to see if the pears are soft and cooked by inserting the tip of a sharp knife. When they are ready, remove the pears from the pan with a slotted spoon and transfer to serving plates.

3. Serve hot with the syrup.

GRILLED FRESH FIGS WITH CRÉME FRAÎCHE

(Serves 4)

Ingredients

- 8 ripe fresh figs.
- 225g/8oz créme fraiche.
- 50g/2oz light muscovado sugar.

Procedure

1. Preheat the grill to high. Lightly butter a shallow flameproof dish, large enough to accommodate the figs in a single layer;
2. Cut the figs into quarters without cutting through the base, and gently open each one out a little. Spoon a dollop of crème fraîche into the centre of each fig;
3. Sprinkle the sugar evenly between the figs. Put the figs in the prepared dish, and put the hot grill for 2 minutes or until the sugar has melted and the crème fraîche starts to run. Serve immediately.

MELON AND ORANGE CUPS

(Serves 4)

Ingredients

- 2 small honeydew melons.
- 1 grapefruit, peeled and segmented.
- 2 oranges, peeled and segmented.
- 50g/2oz roasted, unsalted peanuts.
- 25g/1oz light muscovado sugar.
- 1/4 teaspoon ground cinnamon.

Procedure

1. Halve the melons, scoop out the seeds and discard, then remove and chop the flesh. Reserve the melon shells;
2. In a bowl, mix together the melon and citrus fruits. Pile the fruits back into the melon shells;
3. Chop the peanuts and mix with the sugar and cinnamon. Sprinkle over the fruit and serve.

MELON MEDLEY

(Serves 4)

Ingredients

- 1/2 cantaloupe melon.
- 1/2 honeydew melon.
- 1/2 watermelon.
- pulp from 2 passion fruit.

Procedure

1. Cut the melons into bite-size pieces, or use a melon baller to slice into balls. Chill, covered, for 30 minutes;
2. Drizzle with the passion fruit pulp before serving.

PINEAPPLE & PASSION FRUIT SALSA

(Serves 6)

Ingredients

- 1 small pineapple.
- 2 passion fruit.
- 150ml/5fl oz Greek-style yogurt.
- 2 tablespoons light muscovado sugar.

Procedure

1. Cut the top and bottom of the pineapple. Using a large sharp knife, slice off the peel and remove any remaining 'eyes'. Slice the pineapple, and use a small pastry cutter or an apple corer to remove the tough core from each slice;

2. Cut the passion fruit in half, and scoop the seeds and pulp into a bowl. Stir in the pineapple slices and yogurt. Cover and chill;

3. Stir in the sugar just before serving.

SNOW-CAPPED APPLES

(Serves 4)

Ingredients

- 4 small cooking apples.
- 75ml/3fl oz orange marmalade.
- 2 egg whites.
- 50g/2oz caster sugar.

Procedure

1. Preheat the oven to 180°C/350°F/Gas mark 4.
2. Core the apples and score through the skins around the middle with a sharp knife.
3. Put the apples in a wide ovenproof dish, and spoon 1 tablespoon marmalade into the centre of each. Cover and bake in the oven for 35–40 minutes until tender.
4. Whisk the egg whites in a large bowl until stiff enough to hold soft peaks. Whisk in the sugar, then fold in the remaining marmalade.
5. Spoon the meringue over the apples, then return to the oven for 10–15 minutes. Serve immediately.

RED FRUIT SALAD

Ingredients

- 250g/9oz strawberries, hulled and halved
- 100g/4oz raspberries
- 250g/9oz cherries, pitted
- 1 tablespoon Cointreau
- 1 tablespoon soft brown sugar

Procedure

1. Put the strawberries, raspberries and cherries in a bowl, drizzle with Cointreau, cover and set aside for 20 minutes;
2. Put the sugar and 2 tablespoons water in a small pan. Stir over a gentle heat for 3 minutes or until the sugar has dissolved. Cool, pour over the fruit, and serve.

GRILLED APPLE STACK

(Serves 4)

Ingredients

- 4 large dessert apples, cored and peeled
- 25g/1oz butter
- 1 × 400g/14oz jar lime marmalade
- 4 scoops vanilla ice cream

Procedure

1. Cut the apples into thin slices across the core, and put on a lightly greased grill tray. Top each slice with a small piece of butter and 1/2 teaspoon lime marmalade;

2. Cook under a hot grill until the butter has melted and the apple is golden brown;

3. Serve 4 or 5 slices stacked on top of each other, with a scoop of vanilla ice cream alongside.

GRAPEFRUIT IN APRICOT BRANDY

(Serves 4)

Ingredients

- 3 grapefruit.
- 125ml/4fl oz apple juice.
- 11/2 teaspoons granulated sugar.
- 2.5cm/1in piece of cinnamon stick.
- 3 tablespoons apricot brandy.
- 3 ready-to-eat dried apricots, chopped.

Procedure

1. Cut off all the zest and pith from the grapefruit, working over a shallow pan to catch any juice. Push out the white core using the handle of a teaspoon, then thickly slice the grapefruit;

2. Put the apple juice and sugar in the pan with the cinnamon stick. Bring to the boil, and simmer for 3 minutes. Add the fruit and simmer for 6–8 minutes;

3. Remove the fruit from the pan and transfer to four warmed serving plates. Add the apricot brandy to the juice. Bring back to the boil, then spoon over the fruit and sprinkle with the chopped apricots. Serve immediately.

BLUSHING PEARS

(Serves 6)

Ingredients

- 6 dessert pears.
- 300ml/10fl oz rosé wine.
- 150ml/5fl oz cranberry juice.
- strip of thinly pared orange zest.
- 1 cinnamon stick.
- 4 whole cloves.
- 1 bay leaf.
- 75g/3oz caster sugar.

Procedure

1. Thinly peel the pears with a sharp knife or vegetable peeler, leaving the stalks intact.
2. Pour the wine and cranberry juice into a large heavy pan. Add the orange zest, cinnamon stick, cloves, bay leaf and sugar. Heat gently, stirring all the time, until the sugar has dissolved. Add the pears, standing them upright in the pan. Pour in enough cold water to barely cover them.
3. Cover and cook gently for 20–30 minutes until just tender, turning and basting with the syrup occasionally. Using a slotted spoon, gently lift the pears out of the syrup and transfer to a serving dish.
4. Bring the syrup to the boil, and boil rapidly for 10–15 minutes until it has reduced by half. Strain the syrup and pour over the pears. Serve.

SWEET-STEWED DRIED FRUIT

(Serves 4)

Ingredients

- 500g/1lb 2oz mixed dried fruit salad.
- 450ml/3/pt apple juice.
- 2 tablespoons clear honey.
- 2 tablespoons brandy.
- grated zest and juice of 1 lemon.
- grated zest and juice of 1 orange.

Procedure

1. Put the fruit salad, apple juice, honey, brandy, lemon and orange zests and juices in a small saucepan. Bring to the boil, and simmer for about 1 minute;
2. Remove the pan from the heat, and allow the mixture to cool completely. Transfer to a large bowl, cover with cling film and chill in the refrigerator overnight;
3. To serve, spoon the stewed fruit into four shallow dishes.

GRAPEFRUIT IN APRICOT BRANDY

(Serves 4)

Ingredients

- 3 grapefruit.
- 125ml/4fl oz apple juice.
- 11/2 teaspoons granulated sugar.
- 2.5cm/1in piece of cinnamon stick.
- 3 tablespoons apricot brandy.
- 3 ready-to-eat dried apricots, chopped.

Procedure

1. Cut off all the zest and pith from the grapefruit, working over a shallow pan to catch any juice. Push out the white core using the handle of a teaspoon, then thickly slice the grapefruit;

2. Put the apple juice and sugar in the pan with the cinnamon stick. Bring to the boil, and simmer for 3 minutes. Add the fruit and simmer for 6–8 minutes;

3. Remove the fruit from the pan and transfer to four warmed serving plates. Add the apricot brandy to the juice. Bring back to the boil, then spoon over the fruit and sprinkle with the chopped apricots. Serve immediately.

PEACH MELBA

(Serves 4)

Ingredients

- 300g/11oz fresh raspberries.
- 25g/1oz icing sugar.
- 375g/13oz granulated sugar.
- 1 vanilla pod, split lengthways.
- 4 peaches.
- 4 scoops vanilla ice cream.

Procedure

1. Purée the raspberries and icing sugar together in a blender or food processor. Pass through a sieve and discard the seeds;

2. Stir the sugar, vanilla pod and 600ml/1pt water in a pan over a low heat until the sugar has completely dissolved;

3. Bring the sugar syrup to the boil, and add the peaches, ensuring that they are covered with the syrup. Simmer for 5 minutes or until tender, then remove the peaches with a slotted spoon and carefully remove the skin;

4. To serve, put a scoop of ice cream on each plate, add a peach and spoon raspberry purée on top.

STRAWBERRIES IN GRAPE JELLY

(Serves 4)

Ingredients

- 500ml/18fl oz red grape juice.
- 1 cinnamon stick.
- pared zest and juice of 1 small orange.
- 1 tablespoon powdered gelatine.
- 225g/8oz strawberries, hulled and chopped.

Procedure

1. Pour the grape juice into a pan, and add the cinnamon stick and orange zest. Cook over a very low heat for 10 minutes, then strain the juice and discard the flavourings;

2. Sprinkle the powdered gelatine over the orange juice in a small bowl. When the mixture is spongy, stir into the grape juice until it has completely dissolved.

3. Allow the jelly to cool in the bowl until just beginning to set. Stir in the strawberries, and pour into a 900ml/11/2pt mould. Chill until set.

PERSIAN MELON CUPS

(Serves 4)

Ingredients

- 2 small cantaloupe melons.
- 225g/8oz strawberries, hulled and sliced.
- 3 peaches, peeled and cubed.
- 225g/8oz seedless white grapes.
- 25g/1oz caster sugar.
- 1 tablespoon rose water.
- 1 tablespoon freshly squeezed lemon juice.
- crushed ice, to serve.

Procedure

1. Carefully cut the melons in half and remove the seeds. Scoop out the flesh with a melon baller, taking care not to damage the skin. Reserve the melon shells.
2. Put the strawberries in a large mixing bowl with the melon balls, peaches, grapes, sugar, rose water and lemon juice;
3. •Pile the fruit into the melon shells, and chill in the refrigerator for 2 hours;
4. To serve, sprinkle with the crushed ice, and serve immediately.

NECTARINES WITH MARZIPAN & YOGURT

(Serves 4)

Ingredients

- Nectarines.
- 75g/3oz marzipan.
- 75ml/3fl oz Greek-style yogurt.
- 3 amaretti biscuits, crushed.

Procedure

1. Cut the nectarines in half, removing the stones. Cut the marzipan into 8 pieces, and press one piece into the stone cavity of each nectarine half. Preheat the grill.

2. Spoon the Greek yogurt on top of the nectarines. Sprinkle the crushed amaretti biscuits over the yogurt. Put the fruits under the grill for 3-5 minutes until the yogurt starts to melt. Serve immediately.

GOOSEBERRY

CHEESE COOLER

(Serves 4)

Ingredients

- 500g/1lb 2oz fresh gooseberries.
- finely grated zest and juice of 1 small orange.
- 1 tablespoon clear honey.
- 250g/9oz cottage cheese.

Procedure

1. Top and tail the gooseberries, and put them in a pan. Add the orange zest and juice, and cook gently, stirring occasionally, until the fruit is tender. Remove from the heat and stir in the honey.

2. Purée the gooseberries and their juice in a blender or food processor until almost smooth. Allow to cool.

3. Press the cottage cheese through a sieve until smooth. Stir half of the cooled gooseberry purée into the cottage cheese.

4. To serve, spoon the cheese mixture into four serving glasses. Top each one with gooseberry purée, and serve chilled.

POACHED PEACHES WITH GINGER

(Serves 4)

Ingredients

- 4 peaches, halved and stoned.
- 125ml/4fl oz water.
- 2 tablespoons lemon juice 1cm/1/2 in root ginger, peeled and grated 1 cinnamon.
- Stick.
- 225g/8oz seedless white grapes, halved.

Procedure

1. Preheat the oven to 180°C/350°F/Gas mark 4.

2. Put the peach halves skin side up in a baking dish.;Combine 125ml/4fl oz water, the lemon juice, ginger and cinnamon stick, and pour over the peaches. Poach in the oven for 30 minutes;

3. Remove from the oven and arrange the peaches on four dessert plates. Top with the cooking juices, add the grapes and serve immediately.

FRUIT FONDUE

(Serves 2)

Ingredients

- 50g/2oz soft cheese.
- 150ml/5fl oz hazelnut yogurt.
- 1 teaspoon vanilla essence.
- 1 teaspoon caster sugar.
- selection of fresh fruits for dipping, such as strawberries, satsumas, kiwi fruit, grapes, all cut into bite-size pieces • Beat the soft cheese with the yogurt, vanilla essence and sugar in a bowl.

Procedure

1. Spoon the mixture into a glass serving dish set on a platter. Arrange the prepared fruits around the dip, and serve immediately.

LIME SHERBET

(Serves 6)

Ingredients

- Limes.
- 75g/3oz caster sugar.
- pinch of salt.
- crushed ice, to serve.

Procedure

2. Squeeze the limes and pour the juice into a large jug. Add the sugar and salt. Stir until dissolved • Pour in 1.5 litres/21/2pt water, and top up with plenty of ice to serve.

GRILLED PINK GRAPEFRUIT

(Serves 4)

Ingredients

- 2 pink grapefruit.
- 1 teaspoon granulated sugar.
- 4 scoops vanilla ice cream.

Procedure

3. Halve the grapefruit and cut round the edge of each, between the pith and the flesh. Separate the segments. Sprinkle each grapefruit with sugar.

4. Put in ramekins to keep them flesh side up, and put on a grill pan. Grill for 2–3 minutes until starting to lightly brown. Put a scoop of vanilla ice cream on top of each, and serve immediately.

Thank you for purchasing this recipe book!

If you want to learn more delicious recipes, check the other titles of this series.

Michelle Desire